This Hat

By Eve Feldman

ScottForesman

A Division of HarperCollins*Publishers*

This hat. That hat.
Which hat should I wear?

I wear this hat in the sun.

I wear this hat just for fun.

I wear this hat on a cold day.

I wear this hat when I play.

I wear this hat to look tall.

Hats! I want to wear them all.